becoming

becoming

RHYMES & RUMINATIONS BY

KAT STRAIN

becoming
Copyright © 2024 by Kat Strain.

All rights reserved. This book or any portion thereof may not be reproduced or used in any manner whatsoever without the express written permission of the author except for the use of brief quotations in the context of reviews.

ISBN: 978-1-0689109-4-4

Cover photo by Robert McGee Photography.
robertmcgee.ca

Cover design by Rachel Clift.
Book design & layout by Rachel Clift.
rcliftpoetry.com

First printing edition, 2024.

@sistersstrain
sistersstrain.com
The Sisters Strain

You come and go

So fleeting

All or nothing

Just the same

Even in your absence

You remain

Ready to purge my pain

And the most intimate parts of me

Setting my soul free

And igniting my inner flame

No rhyme or reason

But I've given you a name

My passion, my poetry

~My Adeline~

My heart you contain

prologue

I once had a dream I married a man for legal reasons, and he was accusing me of stealing and lying. I clearly recalled, as I fervently tried to defend my innocence, his referring to me as *Adeline*. Upon waking I discovered the meaning of that name is "noble"- possessing, characterized by, or arising from superiority of mind or character or of ideals or morals…in essence, honourable. Knowing at my core I seek to be as honest and authentic as possible in all ways with my actions and especially my words, *Adeline* became the name for my poet soul.

My compass, my true north, my confessional core.

These words, these worries, these wonders, woes, and wisdom are all hers… and mine. Purged from the plight of this journey we've forged together.

poems

becoming

~The moment I realized I no longer recognized myself. A moody day in LA, numbing with wine to drown my muted misery and convince myself I was happy~

I've felt lost
I've been looking
Searching every corner of my consciousness for the girl I remember
The hope she had
The dreams she dreamt
The plans she made that should have come to fruition by now

But I cannot find her
It seems she no longer exists

Where did she go?
How did she slip so easily through my fingers?

I'm struggling to accept this… this person she's become
To let go of all that has left her and embrace all she has found

It scares and intrigues me
Incites both sadness and joy in my soul

It is mourning and it is anticipation
Looking forward to and dreading leaving behind

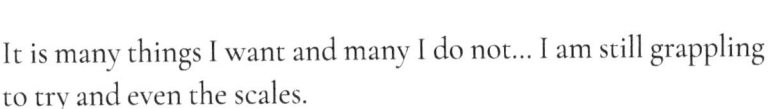

It is many things I want and many I do not… I am still grappling to try and even the scales.

This is when I knew it was time to go home. Not to Toronto, where I lived 10 years prior...but really go home. Tail between legs to the small town I'd forsook the second I was old enough.

I'd given LA all I could and was left with very little to show for it. When you are truly and utterly lost, there's no better place to get found...

becoming

I've shed my skin so many
times I can hardly recognize
myself

Layer upon layer
Recreating, restoring, renewing
Blossoming into something entirely new
while simultaneously rediscovering the roots of who
I've always
been

Like coming home,
but nothing feels the same
and you know it never will be again

And that's okay

My voice started to expand as my mind did too, from succinct poem to lengthy prose. I had a lot more to say than I previously allowed myself to explore. Much more brewing beneath my surface than I was capable of hearing or considering. The quiet contemplation of living in my sister's basement while nannying my niece, caring for her home and acquiring my real estate license unearthed parts of me I had previously been drowning out and denying. At the time, it felt the most shameful and regretful period of my life. I felt a fraud and a failure and had lost every sense of who I was or what I wanted.

Somehow, in the midst of this internal chaos and conflict, I found the truest voice I'd ever known, and my future started to slowly piece together. It was not the one I had imagined, not the dream I originally intended and grasped so many years breathless and bloody knuckled.

And it was not, by any means, an easy road...

But, looking back, it built me a life of such beauty and bliss, it befuddles me to think I ever begrudged it.

becoming

I have always known my soul purpose is to tell stories. I am just realizing more and more that maybe, rather than others, I am meant to tell my own.

It is equal parts terrifying and exhilarating. The vulnerability that comes with reaching deep down to the depths of your person, meddling around and trying to muster some form of magic. The more you dig and the deeper you go, the less you want to know in some ways.
In others the opposite.

It is not comfortable there, it takes courage. But it is alive and electrifying. The more time I spend lost in my depths, the more I find myself. The more myself I become. The more I feel, the more I want to share.
It is a gift.

The best blessing bestowed upon me, this ability to excavate and find the beauty in all my dark little corners and despairing caves. One for which I am grateful every day.

They say you've got to lose yourself to find yourself.

I have done that several times. First outwardly, now inward. I am still searching and exploring. Trying to make sense of what I find. Sometimes I cringe at what stirs beneath my skin, sometimes it fills me with pride.

Either way, I have learned to honour and appreciate every part. Every thought, every feeling, every beautiful or unsightly layer. It all confounds to create the woman I am slowly and purposefully becoming and configures the wonderful, hopeful and heartbreaking stories she will share with the world.

What a lucky lady she is for the luxury to indulge in this labour of love.
I hope she never shallows of these deep dark corners, this curious consciousness or such sumptuous supply of stories to share.

For as long as I can recall, I have been deeply and profoundly moved by literature. I've also had a burning desire to someday be the source of such movement in others.

I numbed myself so long, I shut out every little voice urging me to do so, guiding me to fulfill that desire.
Distracted myself with synthetic love, cheap substances, fake and fickle highs. Fixed myself to feel nothing at all in attempts to dampen the dark. All at the cost of denying myself any true light.

Now that I have ripped off the bandaids and cast aside old crutches, the wells have sprung back to life. Flowing flawlessly, spewing endlessly and effortlessly. There seems to be no sign of staling or stopping, for which I am only too pleased to succumb to this assault. Beyond grateful for the drought of my own devising to be through.

I would gladly and willingly drown in the turbulent oceans of my soul repeatedly than ever again damn my emotions. For better or worse. It is all or nothing. I will take every ounce of decrepit darkness lurking in my depths in exchange for even the slightest sliver of sparkling hope. It is all of value, all of use.

I will never again forsake the ability to feel, to be moved...to heed that little voice that stirs my sensitivities and forces me to sit in my skin and discern every nuance. Respect every emotion. Validate any fleeting thought or feeling at all.

To let it move me. Really move me.

To be moved and to move others in turn.

becoming

Anything can move me these days. I just never know what might touch me or when. I find myself amazed at how beauty and joy can be found in the simplest of things when you really open yourself to it.
When you give yourself permission to.

To be happy, to love life, to let go of anything that impedes you from doing so.

There is freedom in accepting where you are. In giving yourself entirely to the present moment. Wherever that is, whatever it entails. Whatever thought, feeling, or experience you currently find yourself in.

Live it all. Feel it all. Savour it all.

Sometimes it can feel like life takes all you have. And the more you give, the more it continues to take.
Relentlessly.
Give anyway. Be all there anyway. At some point, I promise, it gets easier. Effortless.

I also promise, when it does, you'll get back so much more than you gave.

Sometimes, to gain true clarity on who you are and what you want, you must deny yourself all distraction. After a string of torrid affairs and horrendous heartbreak in Toronto and LA, I decided to take a nice long break from dating. At this point, I was broaching almost a year of celibacy and my energy and intention around love and romance were taking a whole new perspective...

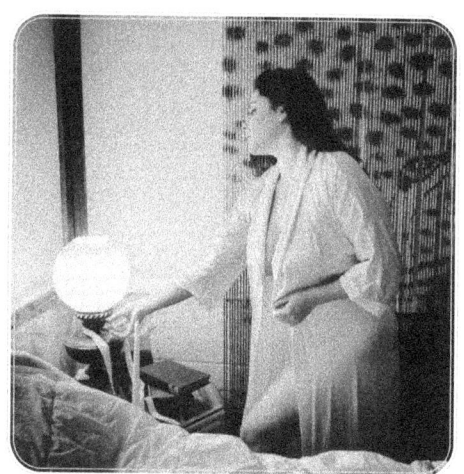

becoming

If you cannot see my soul, do not rest your eyes on my skin. There is nothing for you here.

If you care not to comprehend what is within, then lay your casual glances elsewhere. This body holds nothing for you.

It was not built for your benefit. Its purpose and power will not be determined by the weight of your wonder. Its worth cannot be calculated by its capacity to conjure your concupiscence.

Its qualifications for being of caliber extend far beyond what your eyes convey... regardless of the length at which they should look upon my form.

My curves were not contrived for such careless or callous contemplations.

Do not even consider how they might feel under your caress unless you can commit to uncovering the courses by which they were carved.

If you do not have the proclivity to acquaint yourself with all that they contain... I care not for your considerations.

I cannot curb my cravings on crude inconsequential curiosities.

The concept is inconceivable to be now.

*Only an opulent understanding of my soul could induce any physical ecstasy in me now. Fulfillment of flesh alone would no longer suffice.
Could not truly or thoroughly satiate the hunger that aches at my core.*

I need to be felt and seen in ways that exceed tangible limits.

becoming

Fuck hands.
I am numb to skin deep sensuality.
They could be strong and fair and finesse so fine they render another speechless and I would find myself unaffected.
If your soul is not brushing against my own, my physical form will not feel moved.

Fuck lips.
They have lent me too many lies.
They could be luscious and alluring and linger lengthily in all the right places and still leave me longing.
Warm, wanton kisses will feel cold and chaste to my mouth
if our minds aren't also melding.

Fuck words.
Sweet nothings only steel me for disappointment.
They could be witty and wondrous and whisper the promise of my wildest dreams and I would not be wooed.
Show me your want is unwavering in ways that leave us both wordless.

I'll only hear you with my heart. Speak to me with yours.
Strip me to my soul and stimulate my spirit before you savour my skin.

Arouse me beyond my senses.

I no longer delight in the lithe language of lust…it it's not love, it's just not enough.

kat strain

~It is much easier to be vulnerable with written word than spoken~

becoming

My pen finds the words my tongue stumbles over
I can never quite express what is in my heart through my mouth,
but through my pen my soul has no trouble with clarity

Hear me with your eyes, not your ears
Your ears will never know all that is on my mind,
but your eyes surely will
Listen with those and trust everything they tell you
For they are me, my soul, and my heart
Splayed out in the open

Bare, unencumbered, unabashed, unashamed and unafraid

I never use words lightly
I'd never allow them out of my body unless
I meant them with all my being

Lips easily carry lies
Through them words are given carelessly
Gone the second after they are uttered

But on paper words are eternal
Their weight carried forever
Never forgotten

I only write what I feel enough to mean forever

I will write every word I know, in every possible way,
to tell you the extent of my love for you
And pray you hear them
Believe them
And one day return them
Unencumbered, unabashed, unashamed and unafraid
Mean them enough to seal them in ink

Write me your heart, let me hold it forever
You already have mine

I am slowly becoming the woman I have wanted to be for quite a while. I had to first create and kill countless other versions of her. They are ghosts to me now. A bit of each still beat in me, somewhere, but I will never fully exist as any ever again. Their tales, trials and triumphs built me. Piece by piece.

Every broken heart, every big leap, every rejection, false hope and failed attempt.

becoming

I did not love most of those women. I barely tolerated a few. The ones I despised ended up being the hardest to let go. At times, I truly believed I did not want to.

There is a certain comfort in lingering in misery. A sweet absolution from the hard work it takes to pull yourself out of it. To admit you want more. To demand more. It's not easy to release your limitations. It's far too comfortable to just remain in them. You simply cannot fail if you lay no claims to what you crave at your core.

Excuses will bury you alive if you let them. They will blind you to the point where you cannot see the possibility of better. You can convince yourself you are thriving. That things are as good as they get.

It's amazing how little you can live off. The scraps you accept when struggling becomes the standard. You cannot recognize the lack in such an existence until you finally stand outside of it. Until you finally make the hard choices, forge the difficult change.

All those shadows of myself feel like a world away now. It's tough to imagine ever assuming their skin. But I am grateful to each. For all the things they found in the dark and all the fires they braved to bring me light.

I love that we are always evolving. Rearranging and renewing. Forever. We can change any time we choose, to whatever we decide.

I look forward to all the versions of myself I will proudly stand in one day, but no longer miss the ones I have shed. I know, too, the woman I now inhabit will be fleeting so I will cherish her every breath.

She is brave and bold in who she is and what she wants, and I am in love with all she is becoming.

Though I was studying a new career and embracing this new life, my heart still yearned for success in my art. I could not shut it off or tune it out. I poured every particle of my soul and each moment I could spare into keeping the dream alive. Waking up at dawn to study other poets and authors while writing my first screenplay and sending off audition tapes in hopes something might still swoop in and save me from the life of monotony I saw splayed before me.

Each rejection along with the pressure to let this go and pursue other endeavours weighed heavy on my heart and chipped away at my steely resolve...

becoming

She has rested far too long on her resilience. Accepting much less than she knows she deserves. Quietly conceding while her body burns to dare and defy. Simply living will no longer suffice, she wants to thrive.

She is strong but shouldn't have to be. Brave, but for how long? Courageous, but at what cost? She has given too many inches for miles taken against her will.
Taken for granted.

Sure, she'll bounce back. Yes, she'll get over it and forge ahead…she is resilient.

But why should she have to be? When does it relinquish to respected? Radiant? Relevant?

She has been the "good girl". Does the right deeds, says the right words and tries repeatedly, relentlessly.
Resigns herself to the crude realities of the world and graciously accepts her defeats.

"Don't be crazy. Don't cry or make a fuss. Work harder, do better…I'm sure you'll get the next one."

But she is restless and ravenous and can feel the façade beginning to falter. The righteous sting of rebellion scorches her insides. Her blood is liquid fire. It is rampant and reckless, and she refuses to restrain its rush.

And should her resilience finally give way to the ruthlessness that rips at her withering resolve… there's just no saying what will ruin in the wake of her wrath.

kat strain

The life of an artist can feel like hardly living at all...

becoming

Those who make the world more vivid for others rarely enjoy their own so vivaciously. We spend our days holding our breath, waiting for the other shoe to drop… waiting for our life to begin. The struggle a searing slight against the joy and pride our work insights. Especially when most only deem our essence valuable once it is monetized. Once we have "made it" …we are making it every day. It's a call that never ceases. No free moments, no days off. We are felt so deeply by others due to the depths of which we ourselves feel. Most often those feelings aren't pleasant. We endure them patiently; pray they pass and paint them prettily before presenting them to the world. Putting our pain on a pedestal and hoping it worthy of your praise and not your pity. Little shards of our soul on offer to be rejoiced or rejected on a whim.

And then wait and wait, for our life to begin.

We can't just revel in the release of our passion; we must pray it proves a profit. Then it will have worth and be worth our time. Worth committing our life to. Worth living for. But any artists know it was never a choice. It's as natural an urge as our brain signaling our lungs to breath. As essential to our survival.
This life chose us, and we must live it the only way we know how. On rare occasion it's even, most times it's depleting. Giving, purging, producing. For nothing in return. We give anyway. Try and try again.

Maybe this time we'll convince them, and our life will finally begin.

"Don't be so sensitive. Get a thicker skin. You need to work harder, maybe do something else instead." Never quite appreciated for our ability to let things in. To feel, to be affected and turn it into art for your benefit. We can callous our skin, but our souls won't give in. We can't cure our creativity or shield our sensitive proclivities. We were born to be porous. To seek fulfillment not fame. To brave this gift, in all its beauty and shame. To share it with the world despite the weight or worth of our name. To be killed and birthed repeatedly and make poignant our perilous pain.

To blaze brilliantly, burn out and begin again, again and again.

Inspired by the only bud-less tree outside my window...

Barren branches beckon
Brown brittle fingers from above
Reaching, clawing
For something beyond their clutch

Backdropped by a bland grey sky
Bleak, bereft
The robin bobbing with the breeze
The only sign of life

It becomes me
Boisterous, boundless
Clinging to a wasteland
Willing it bring me skyward

Bated in bitterness and begrudging this beam on which
I've blithely balanced my ambitions

becoming

Frustration seeps through every pore
I bare my soul; they just ask for more

Ten years of risk, still no reward
No length I haven't gone or avenue unexplored

I pour my heart on the floor
Yet so easily ignored

On days like this I wonder what I'm fighting for
Have I had enough? Can I take anymore?

And why must my foolish heart be so damn sure...

I can't quit this

kat strain

*Written for a terribly wrong person, but I like the notion
and hope to feel these words someday...*

I've never seen you in the flesh, yet you've captured my soul

I get this sense I'd find safety in your arms and home in your eyes

I do not know you but feel you could be mine, my other half,
a kindred kind
Someone I could really count on this time
Could it be that simple, cause baby you're blowing my mind

Got me longing for your love, to let our souls entwine
To stand in your presence and finally feel fully alive
To take on this world side by side, shed the skins of our past,
forge forward and thrive
My heart is open and available if you should be so inclined
If you give me yours, I could grant you mine...
Let's fall in love

becoming

Getting back on the horse is never easy...

I have learned not to put much stock in those who are too quick with their affections. They'll offer you the sky with no intention of giving it to you. Convince you it's already yours and watch you free fall without a safety net.

Pay you pretty words, feed you fanciful notions and beguile you with illusions of grandeur. They'll know all the right things to say and the exact moments to do so. Swoop you away and strand you on a whim. Build you up as quickly as they burn out and leave you confused, questioning yourself and clambering to catch your breath.

Nothing quite qualms the salty sting of realizing you've opened to someone you shouldn't have. Someone you believed safe to show your sensitivities and certain would cherish them.

The more I attempt to share my soul, the more spiteful I become. The more I want to shield myself and the softness I worked so hard to cultivate. I have spent years sanding smooth my rough edges and chiseling away my calloused encasing. Slowly learning to accept my softness as a strength rather than a shortfall.

I cannot fathom how anyone could be so fickle with their affections. So flippant with their feelings or so cruel in their carelessness. I despise the resentment spurned by such scorn. My compulsion is to slip back into the old familiar safety of my jaded, hard-hearted façade.

The slightest shift in energy will have me recoil without a second thought. I've become hypersensitive to inconsistency. Weary of promises made without proven intentions. It leaves me doubting the existence of any truly trustworthy and authentic souls. Convinced no one will ever see and celebrate my soft spirit and trust me with theirs.

Will I ever be able to bare myself to another without begrudging the burn of regret? Will I ever be able to love without doubt, shame or apprehension...without the fear of feeling stupid?

Every beat of my battered heart wants to believe it exists, but I've yet to behold it. I want to stay soft, stay open, but each blow stings just a little bit worse than the last... bittering my benevolence and harrowing any hopes held by this helpless romantic.

kat strain

I am tired of being resilient.

Tired of being disappointed, of expecting disappointment.
Of walking on eggshells, tepidness and tip toeing around uncertainty.

I want to not be afraid or ashamed of my feelings
and trust another to share them with.
No limitations.

I am tired of timid baby steps; I want bounds and leaps.
I want to blindly fall all in and revel in its unbridled bliss.

I want clear, unwavering, undoubtedly returned love, respect, admiration and adoration. I want to be cherished by a soul I cherish in return. I want softness and sweet nothings, not callousness, questioning and cruelty.

I want to feel that excitement build and not hold my breath,
waiting for it to burst like it always does.

I have so much to give and wish I could give it. I truly do. I wish someone wanted it so explicitly that they knew they couldn't possibly live without it once they got a taste. Wouldn't even try to test its limits or parallel it in another.

I want passion and intimacy.

I must believe romance isn't dead. I feel it so strongly to my depths.
Swirling around, longing to be shared…
but wasted, like my body and soul in the best years of my life.

I want to fall head over heels. I want to fall with my whole heart.
I want to fall without feeling fucking foolish.

More than anything. I just want to fall.

becoming

Midnight musings...

It's 2am
I am awake and the silence is deafening
My heart pounds in my head
In tandem with the cat curled to my side
Keeping warm my bed
Lulling me to sleep with her sweet purr
This little beast won't be here forever
Who will warm me then?
The minutes tick by slowly giving way to the hour
And still, here I lay
Soothed by her soft sigh...yet sleepless

Contemplations as I approached the end of my education and the beginning of my new career as a real estate agent. My life, finances and future more stable and promising than ever...yet still, I struggled.

becoming

Sometimes I think I am scared of success. I wouldn't know what to do with it were I to stumble upon it tomorrow. I've lived in the safe space of failure for so long. It is comfortable. It is easy. It cannot let me down.

I've spent so much of my life reaching and chasing that I do not know what I would even do if I actually caught all the things I wanted. If I held them in my hands. If I could touch them, taste them, claim them for my own.

They terrify me.

Life has shown me repeatedly how unready and unworthy I am for so many dreams that were I to stand in their presence I'm not sure I would be able to even accept them.

How will I feel when there is nothing left to chase, nothing more to prove? I have dug myself into and clawed my way out of so many pits that solid steady ground seems absurd.

Impossible.

What if I had it all? Everything I want. Every wish, every dream, every hope?

Am I worthy? Am I ready? Do I even want those things at all?

To not struggle, to breath freely, to live fully,
to not second guess or question my next step...what a gift that would be.
What a beautiful blessing indeed.

So why, when I'm standing so close, am I shaken more than ever before?

I am the safest I have ever been...yet I have never known such fear.

Lonely girl in the sunset...

I sat beneath the rays of the evenings golden sun,
and I too felt radiant.

Warm, electric, unstoppable.
Like nothing could stand in my way.
The day was mine and I had yet to make it.

Then, like a tiny seed germinating in my soul,
loneliness sprouted.
That familiar empty feeling.

All is bliss under the suns bright light,
but there will be no one to illuminate my night.

No one to love me, make me feel alright.
Laugh and dance under the moonlight.
Drink wine, make me shine and hold me tight.

*When the sun gleams, so too do I.
When it slips below the horizon,
it steals my heart with it.*

*Leaving me and the moon
to share in our secret solitude.
Pale and partial proxies
of their previous presence.*

*If the sun saw me then...
it would not recognize me.*

becoming

*I have chased a lot of things
for a very long time...*

*Dreams, places, people.
The idea of what I wanted
or thought my life should be.*

*I don't want to chase anymore.
I won't.*

I will always confidently go after the things I want, the things that are important to me, but I won't convince them to want me back.

I don't know how to be coy.
I am not scared to hold my heart in my hand and take a chance.
That part of myself I could never change.
I would not want to.

But I won't hold it out in earnest when sincerity is wavering or unreturned. It is open, apparent and available and its worth does not need to be proven.

I've spent the better part of my life worrying, wondering and trying to force answers and understanding. That only ever got me further from the things that I wanted. Confusing the questions that burn in my soul and lengthening the longings that stir in my heart.

I must believe the things I am waiting and hoping for are out there waiting and hoping for me too.
With the same conviction.
The same ferocity.
And when we finally find each other there will be no questions,
no doubt, no convincing.

Just a sigh of relief and the calm comfortable feeling of coming home.

The whispers that woke me in the wee hours of the morning...

My heart feels about a thousand pounds.
Dense in its capacity to love...held heavy by its stagnation.
I long to pour it into another.
To share this burden.
To release this tether. Be free and light.
Give easily and endlessly.

I was blessed with such bountiful love and cursed
with no one to bestow it upon.
I am convinced I could burst if I must continue to carry it alone.

Hold out your hands and I will fill them.
I promise they will never again feel empty.

This love could cure what ails you, if given the chance it could save us both.

becoming

I am Irish built
I'm no withering rose
My soul is soft
But my body will impose its presence

I am fire and water
Two worlds collide
A raging storm or wildfires rush
A drowsy drizzle and a candles flickering glow

~Whether I soothe or scorch, I'll make damn sure I am felt~

I'll never tame the lungs of my lioness
Or coax my crab from its coveted shell
I can be the life of the party
Or the lonesome loser just as well

My telltale heart is incapable of a lie
It is big and beseeching
Worn on my sleeve
Nothing to hide, no reason to deceive

~It may be sweet, but do not dare misconceive it for being weak~

I used to begrudge the breadth of my frame
My stocky limbs and solid stature
Now I admire it
And appreciate its strength

A man once called me thick
Thinking it a compliment
I felt ashamed
But I've learned over the years to see it his way

~It's carried me through many courses, braved a lot of pain~

I'll never have a 24" waist or a gap between my thighs
But I have a pure heart
And kindness in my eyes
To me that is worth more

I've stopped smoothing my hair
Left my wild waves untamed
I prefer my skin natural
See no need to paint my face

~How I am seen on the surface holds no weight to how I feel at my core~

I've donned and discarded many masks
Bit my tongue and swallowed my words
I'll never again deny my truth
From myself nor the world

I won't hush my voice
Turn my cheek or minimize myself
Sacrifice my sincerity or comfort
For the sake of someone else

~I'll always be kind but not at the cost of "staying in line" or being a "good girl"~

I've sanded my edges
Softened my soul
After the weight of the world took its toll
I'll never callous myself again

My mood rises with the sun
Recedes when the clouds roll in
I can be sensitive and messy
But I am a trustworthy friend

~I promise the prick of my thorns is worth the perfume of my petals~

I am not perfect, but I am me
Unapologetically, authentically
I value my integrity
Love deeply and unconditionally

I am proud of my imperfections
And unafraid to love fearlessly
I will not censor my soul
Nor accord it recklessly

~I'm no withering rose…I've no desire to be~

becoming

An amorous analogy...

They say you should never lend money unless you can afford to lose it.

I think the same goes for love.

Love is always a bit of a gamble. A risk. Giving with no guarantee of getting the same in return.
It is not even always about what you get back per-se. But it is not possible to give from a place of lack.

I am coming to terms with the fact that, although I feel the stirrings of loneliness and a deep longing for love, my soul is not truly in a place where it could afford to lose any more. It cannot give any more of itself without a return on its investment.

I have hurt deeply. I have healed and mended many wounds. Grown stronger, wiser, surer. But I am just not ready to take that leap.

My heart is strong but fragile...I cannot conceive of lending it to another.
It simply could not sustain the loss.

I have seen the beauty in far too many beasts.
Been blinded by my belief in benefit of the doubt and burnt because of it.

becoming

I have learned not everyone is deserving of your love, your light, your affection.

I do believe people are inherently good. Certainly no one is all bad, but intention can be a fickle and funny thing. Easily mistaken. Too often boasted for more that it can bear.

My soul was born to see the beauty in all others. It is a blessing I do not begrudge. But I have learned brevity in setting and respecting boundaries. Honouring my own heart and not bartering its peace and purity for another.

It can be difficult to discern upon who we should bestow the bounty of our beautiful little hearts. I can so easily be filled with so much love for so many things. At times, practically brimming.

The tiniest flint can set my soul aflame. I want to burst, to bathe the world in my bliss, to breath such beauty into another. To fill their lungs and set their soul ablaze.

But not everyone desires such heat. Not everyone can handle it.

Many have feared my flames and besmirched my ability to burn. Doused my fire and scorned its ashes. Left me smoldering and second guessing myself. I have burned for many unwilling to burn for me.
I have rested, restored, rekindled and continued to blaze. Bore the brunt of many a beast and still believe in beauty.

At some point, I am bound to find someone to stoke rather than smother my flames. A soul brave enough to set themselves on fire and burn just as fearlessly. And I will know exactly why I had to endure such excessive extinguishing.

To learn to forsake any flame lesser than my own and be able to recognize a force as fierce. To not feel resignation or recoil at the wildfires rush when it is upon me, but blaze brilliantly beside it. To not settle with lukewarm embers of a fleeting spark but hold out for the raging inferno of my twin flame.

And when we both finally catch fire, when I feel that heat...I will know what it is to truly burn...and the blaze will be worth every belittling blight.

If no one is here to look upon my face and tell me so... Am I still beautiful?

Without a handsome sir to admire my form in appreciation...
Am I still desirable?

Should no publisher deem my words worthy of print...
Can I still call myself a writer?

If I should never again be compensated for it...
Am I still an artist?

Validation is a fickle mistress and most untrustworthy companion,
yet we all crave her so and abhor her absence.

Deep down we all need her...and she knows it.

becoming

Covid was tough on us all and I was not spared. I had packed on an extra 20-30 pounds of weight but was slightly in denial about it...this certainly opened my eyes.

Last time I saw my grandmother
She reduced me to tears
She looked at me pensively
Hadn't seen me in years

I had hoped in pride
And joy at my return
Instead, she shook her head
Disappointed, concerned

At what had become
Of her "beautiful little doll"
Repeatedly uttering the words
My mind regrets to recall

"I just cannot believe how much weight you've put on"

This caught me off guard
And cut me deeply
Though not intended with malice
It hurt me needlessly

No care about my health
Or the journey I'd been through
But rather the shape of my body
And the ways in which it grew

In a recent disagreement
With an old, disgruntled friend
Among various other insults
She was quick to offend

"You could stand to lose some weight"

Again, without warning
I was stricken with shame
These words meant to sting
To purposely cause pain

Like salt in a wound
I thought I'd mended
Shattering my resolve
My confidence upended

Despite all you do
To thicken your skin
It's funny how words
Can still weasel their way in

How swiftly their venom
Can leave your heart infected
So carelessly uttered
So thoughtlessly injected

Yes, I have changed
My thin form has filled out
I am no "little doll"
But a woman, no doubt

The size of a person's body
Is no one else's business
It baffles me one would think
To so brazenly offer their opinion

I'm the healthiest I've ever been
Both mentally and physically
Has nothing to do with my dress size
Or how I'm perceived externally

becoming

These days the weight of my words
Hold much more worth to me
Than the weight I carry on my bones
Or the size of my jeans

I've put more stock in the fullness of my heart
And less in the breadth of my body
I take pride in who I am, be it size 2 or 10
That should not matter to anyone who truly cares for me

Found this in my notes. A little musing I wrote on my first New Year's Eve back in Canada...

No kiss at midnight, no clubs, no shimmering dress...no one to hold me and wish me the best.

I got drunk with my brother-in-law, not related by blood but the closest of kin, and rang in the new year dancing with the best of them...my niece, my heart, my new best friend.

So happy to be here, so far from where I have been.

The joy in her eyes, a smile so wide, nothing could compare or leave me more satisfied.

becoming

Mother nature can unburden, release, rage, alter and state her case any damn time she pleases. She is honoured, revered, admired and respected for it.

We call it nature.
Natural.

Yet deem it unacceptable, monstrous, repulsive and "unfeminine" when by that very nature, a woman should do the same.

I haven't written anything in days, and it fills me with dread…with fear that I have no more words to offer the world.

For once my emotions are stable. I am at peace. Nothing is shaking my soul or causing me strife. And that's a good thing. That should be a good thing.

Yet, I cannot help but wonder if all I have to offer has already been uttered. In purging the pain and mending my wounds, have I lost my muse?

Can I only create from darkness? From misery?

In feeling good, have I lost the essence of this self I have come to know and love… the parts of me I take most pride in?

I cannot help but worry the wondrous well has finally run dry. That my once wild and raging heart has been bled all it may, and as such suddenly turned to stone.

I am no stranger to loneliness. I have lived with it as my solo companion quite a while now. But I at least had expression to keep me warm at night. To shed light on my days. To satisfy and soothe my shaken soul.

Those wounded words, haunting thoughts and errant emotions…

What am I without them?

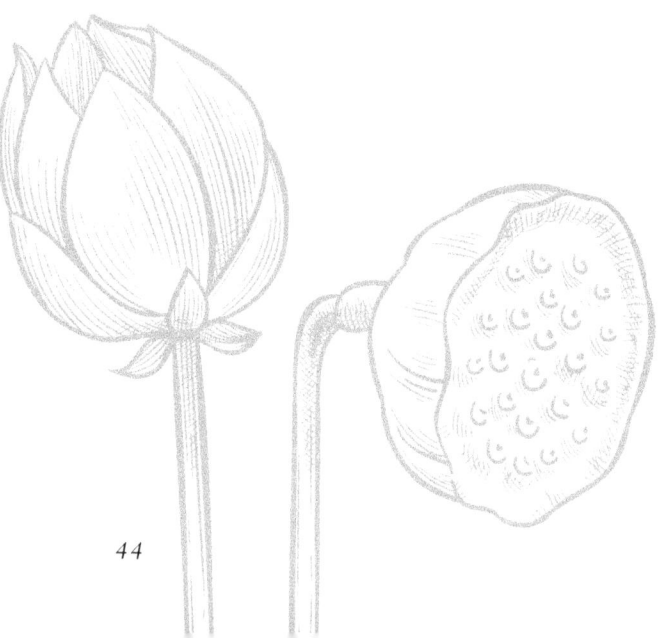

becoming

My eyes hide behind thick dark frames today
Concealing the emotions swimming within them
I am not sure I have any right to be as sad as I feel in this moment
I can't even be certain of its cause
I just know it currently consumes me and I crave its release

To revel in it just a moment
To feel its weighted burden slide down my cheek warm and wet
To sense the salt of its sting and know I am truly alive

That my heart still beats, my eyes still well,
and I am still capable of such ardent affliction

For so long I have built my identity around a sense of longing...
of missing and wishing, hoping while living without.

Having and belonging are foreign territory for my timorous feet.

I am still slowly learning how to confidently stride their steady terrain.

becoming

Something happens to females around 30, as my grandmother pointed out. Your body seems to shift over night. From girl to woman. Full where things used to be flat and slightly softer where previously quite supple. Added to the tab of my already overwhelming identity crisis...I have no doubt my experience is not unique!

I put on a dress today. An old favourite I have always loved and have not worn in years. It carried some once cherished memories, now a burden to my soul. Today seemed like a good day to break those bonds and build new ones.

My figure filled it flawlessly. Like a glove. As though it were made from my exact measurements.

And yet, as I fastened the last button and took in my reflection, I immediately felt deflated. "It doesn't fit anymore," I thought. It used to and now it doesn't. I was upset. I wanted to rip it from my limbs and toss it to the back of my closet. Disgusted by the ways in which my body was betraying me.

The last time I had donned it, 5 years younger and 20 pounds lighter, it was on the verge of too big. I belted it at the waist and left a few buttons open at the bust to prove I did indeed have a figure under the baggy garment.

That is how I remember it. Feeling thin and feminine and loving the way it hung off my frame.

The way it "fit".

The first time I wore it for the benefit of a beloved, he took me in long and deep, admiration clearly evident on his face. Compliments offered freely and plentifully for how beautiful I looked in it.

I looked at myself now, certain any eyes that might behold me would not carry the same appreciation.
That no compliments would roll off any tongue that took me in.

I forced myself to wear it anyway.
Doing my best to embrace this more voluptuous version.

But all morning, as my last button pulled each time I sat at my desk with my hips stressing the seams, I felt my composure fray. My sense of self confidence as strained as the fabric adorning my formidable figure. Resentment simmering in the back of my brain, shame searing the pit of my stomach. I wanted to retch. I wanted to curl up in a ball and hide from the world.

I so desperately wanted to look in the mirror and see the girl I remember looking back at me. The reflection I loved. Her youthful face and thin form burnt into my brain as a skewed perception of beauty and worth...the one I can't seem to let go of. The one that will never exist again. Could never exist again.

She is a ghost. A fragment of my imagination. Her thoughts, her form, her hopes and dreams-none of them exist anymore. None of them are my own.

So why do I continue to give her such space in my mind? Why do I let my opinion of my self, my body, my sense of value be shaped by her outdated ideals and standards. They are irrelevant. She is irrelevant.

She has grown.
In wisdom, in strength, in spirit and in shape.

The dress fits. It just doesn't fit the way it used to. Because I am not who I used to be. I have grown into the dress and outgrown that body, that mindset and its limitations.

We have all been here. We all wrestle the remains of our past selves. We all know, deep down, it is foolish. But that certainly doesn't keep that pesky little voice from pecking away at our self-possession. It certainly doesn't make it any easier to drown out those fears and doubts when they creep in and consume our otherwise confident, rational and reasonable selves.

Damn those long lost, yet ever lingering ghosts.
But we are human...we all just need a little exorcism from time to time

becoming

*This one was actually written while I was still living in LA,
days before my impending 30th birthday.
Also inspired by a dress. Same girl, same body but different perspective...*

I have been reflecting a lot on my 20's. All the ways I took the health and fitness of my young, resilient body for granted. How I rolled my eyes at older women who warned me it would change in the blink of any eye as I got older. I'd always been very confident in the way I felt about how I looked in my body but less so in the way I felt about and loved the person and soul my body encased.

The last few years have been a wild ride. Turbulent to say the least. Mentally and emotionally. I've learned a lot, grown a lot and found a confidence, pride in, and love for myself as a person that I never thought possible. In focusing on the work I needed to do inside, the outside seemed a lot less important. Suddenly, I can understand those kind warnings of my youth. My body has changed in so many ways.

Some days I love every damn inch of her and others I hardly recognize her as my own. It is a tough balance to regain control while also learning to accept and embrace change.

BUT…sometimes you capture yourself in the right angle, or outfit/mood and it does not matter if your arms look fat, how much cellulite you have on your ass or if your stomach roll is showing because you feel entirely, authentically yourself in every possible essence.

Those moments are rare and beautiful and worth treasuring.

I haven't had many of those lately…but today I did.

becoming

Some days I am softer than others...

It is something I struggle to embrace
To celebrate and not shy away
I have steeled myself so long to the worlds wicked ways
I long to shed those walls and be unafraid
To bask in the glow of my souls sweetest rays
To share them with the world and not feel ashamed

I have hardened my heart
Now I must smooth its edges
Sand its rough surface
Release old encumbrances
Stand in this thickened skin
Feel the strength that swells within

And accept its seminal source IS my softness

If living with my sister seemed a tough adjustment, I had no idea the toll moving back in with my parents at 32 would take. But here I was in my small hometown of Chatham Ontario, single, armed with a realtor's license, set to join my fathers team and living under my parents roof...the next few years would be a wild ride.

becoming

Growing up I could never feel settled here. I was always too consumed by lofty thoughts of all the possibilities the world held and dreams of someday holding them once I had the freedom to.

I never imagined coming back. I was sure I would find everything I couldn't quite explain but knew surely must exist and more. Sure the world would meet and exceed the expectations my little heart held sacred.

I let my feet lead me many places in search of these treasures. I let my heart pull me into and out of many arms in attempts to feel I belonged. I let my mind build the biggest dream bubbles and felt them slowly deflate under the weight of reality.

The more I chased, the less I found. The more I grasped the unattainable, the easier it seemed to slip through my fingers and slide away.

I'm not even quite certain what I am looking for these days. But I know I won't find it anywhere other than in myself.

Perhaps that is why I can sit in this place and not itch or fret. Why I can hold this time without my fingers burning to reach and grab for more…for different…for better.

I am more, I am different, and I am better.

I hold in my heart the possibilities of all my wildest dreams.

Where I am does not matter.

I already posses everything I spent so many years chasing…perhaps I always did.

I spent my 20's barrelling through the process to get to the purpose. The meaningfulness. Not realizing the process is part of it.

Holding my breath and sleepwalking through the steps, the every day, to get to the end game...the finish line...the point where I am happy and successful.

Keeping people and places at arms length. Never wanting to get too close to anyone or anything. Not wanting to be tied down or held back.

I don't think I really ever realized just how detached I was or what it denied me.

I have finally accepted that this allusive aspiration does not exist.

This is it. This is all it is. Every step, every breath.
That is the beauty, that is the joy.

I am no longer living for "just in case", "someday", or "until then".

It is a different life, to live fully present.

To be all in exactly where I am.

To sit in it, feel it, embrace it...live it fully.

That's life.

That is what we are here for, folks.

becoming

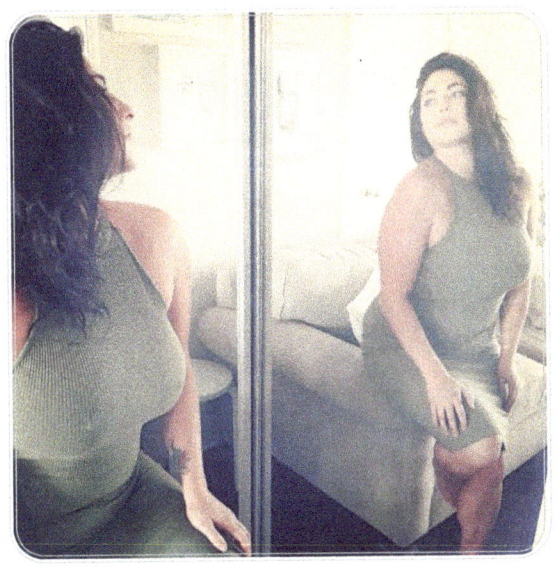

I truly believe my mind is much more interesting than my body, yet I find myself appreciated merely for my curves and not my curiosities...

kat strain

Some may wish to run their hands along my surface,
but few dare delve deeper than my skin.

My thoughts carry much more allure than my form yet remain unchartered.

A quick discovery to any who care to wander within.

My lips grow weary, for if given the chance, they could stimulate more sumptuously by speaking rather than simply resting against another's.

My hands long to stir and sooth creatively in ways that are lasting and can be felt by the world...beyond the carnal pleasures they could extend for one evening.

My passions are pensive, deeply rooted in my bones,
fully expressed through more than just physical prowess.

My linguistic lust should illicit more longing than what lay between my legs.

I care not for compliments on my eyes from those who've never really,
truly looked into them.

If searched, you would see my soul.

Once acquainted, you would no longer slake yourself on my shell alone.

becoming

Woven into the last whisps of a dream and recorded upon waking...

I am not saying I don't want to be considered sexy.

I do.

I just want to be seen as soft, sweet, and spirited too.

Why can't I be both?

The early hours of the day brought me great sadness and these words...

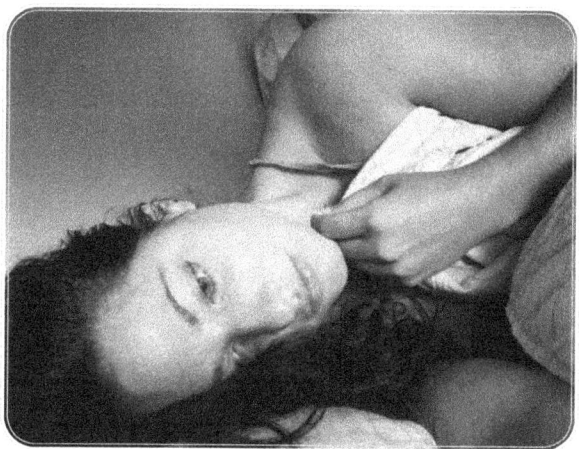

This morning I woke very early. I lay there a while, startled by the emptiness of my bed. Thinking how nice it would be to share it with another. To feel the heat of their embrace and be soothed by the sound of their pulse in the dark.

To know love. To be loved. To pour my passion into another and feel it undoubtedly returned. To share such a soft moment with the solace of a safe soul.

Most days I am fine with being alone. Most days I do not feel entirely lonely. I have known this solitude so long I scarcely take stock of it anymore.

But sometimes, in quiet moments like this, while the world sleeps and there are no distractions to quiet my thoughts, I am consumed. I long to hold and be held. To feel and be felt. To give all and receive another's.

In moments like this but one question haunts my mind and keeps me from slumber.

Where are you love...do you not long for me too?

becoming

At times I feel so full I could burst…others so hollow I am astounded I still stand.

As ever, my weary heart beats to the steady rhythm of resilience.

The world is filled with such fickle beings.

Open one instant, gone the next.

No care extended to consider another beyond superficial assumptions.

I have been fooled on many occasions but flippant never once with my affections.

It's not surprising I am so fruitless in my attempts to find solace in another soul.

I am a summer storm when the sky turns grey. You can see and feel me clearly.

I leave no room for doubt.

I am the year long summer of the California state.

You need not fear a change in my seasons.

The endurance of my love, once earned, is unending. It will not wither or stray.

My heart is on my sleeve and my eyes do not dare deceive.

Be it smooth sailing or a raging rush, you shall only ever find safety in my seas.

I require very little to keep content.

Yet, all too easily and often, I am quickly forwent.

kat strain

The geese fly by in a scattered "V"
Their wanderlust calls to me
I too feel the urge to migrate
To spring from these feet

To soar amidst the stars
From this earth be free
To gain a new perspective
From the tops of the trees

To surrender my fate to the wisdom of my wings.

becoming

The days tick by, turning weeks to years
My passion dries while time extends

In my prime and wasted
Utterly wasted

Too much to give and no one to relieve me of the burden

kat strain

The warm remembrance of a once fervent flame...

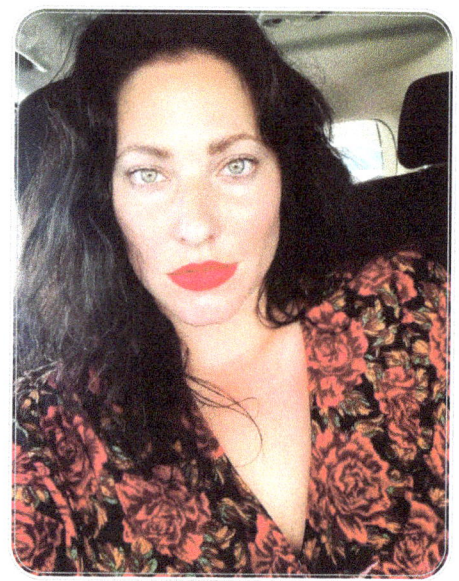

It is those memories
I revisit when I need
to feel alive

To remind myself
what it feels like
to burn with passion,
to give without restraint,
to love fearlessly,
and want without shame

I can only pray, one day, I'll know such pleasure again

becoming

I remember that feeling of safety...of being saved last year when I moved back home to my parents from LA. Not previously having realized I needed saving.

I vividly recall sitting in the shower with the water running, feeling empty and directionless. Full of grief and uncertainty. Just praying and pleading for help, for guidance...for a different life.

Now, here I sit once again a year later. Same tub, overcome with the same intensity of emotion. This time of gratitude. Filled with pride in and love for this life I get to live every day. I helped myself, guided myself...saved myself.

I am thankful every day for the little voice that finally slipped through my veneer of contentedness and begged me to return home.

Thankful I had a home to return to.

I haven't quite found all I seek, but I am no longer lost. I can breathe easy; I can build and live my life. I have structure and stability...foreign concepts to the shambled years of my 20's.

I do not have it all, but I am damn grateful for that which I do.

I have been thinking a lot about LA today. Endless days of sunny warmth yet shrouded in misery. Dark and desperate. Filled with fear and doubt.

Today was the first snowfall. I took the dogs for a walk on the open country roads and icy slush pelted my skin. Pins and needles in my numb face and a deep shiver down my spine.

Then my mind drifted to LA. Bright, balmy LA. Despite the cold, I did not wish for those days. I'll take snow and sleet and winters cold and bleak over that meaningless existence.

I'd gladly trade rain over returning to that sort of pain ever again...

Dear LA,

I think of you in November
On cold miserable days

And still...

I do not miss you
Or smile at the mention of your name

I've no wish to return
Or let you steal more of my days

I do not reminisce your beauty,
Only think of you with shame

Of your coldness and your cruelty
And the dreams you stripped away

And for all the little ways
I let you berate and betray
My hopeful heart

becoming

Nothing festers worse than unreleased wounds from past relationships...

4 years now since we have been done
And I still hate you for all the ways
You broke my heart and betrayed my trust
Using me for your benefit and calling it love
I gave you my all and it was never enough

And I hate myself even more
For believing you were the one
For not seeing the warnings
And ignoring the urge to run
For concealing the pain
By sweeping it under the rug
And convincing myself it doesn't still cut

You took all I had and gave nothing for free
Your love came with strings
While mine was offered unconditionally
I was a fool for you
You made a fool out of me
Did all I could to build you up
And you kept taking until I was empty

I betrayed myself repeatedly
In attempts to make you happy
You took my softness for granted
And used it against me
Shattered my sense of worth
Made me ashamed of my sensitivity
I trusted you completely
And you lied like it was easy

I like to think I've moved on
That I am healed and fully free
But those wounds are deep
And they are begging to breathe
I guess its time to acknowledge
Accept and release
But I still struggle to find forgiveness
For all the little ways you destroyed me

I have been thinking a lot about 27. Who I thought I was, what I thought I wanted...how close I believed I was to holding those things.

Something about today feels similar, sitting at almost 32. Despite all the time and growth in between. It's truly crazy how time flies. How you don't even feel it while it's slipping away and suddenly it's years later and as though you have only taken a small step. Funny how life works out. As they say, seems the more things change the more they stay the same.

I still feel like that girl mostly. Her bright dreams, her burning desires, her big restless heart and defiant spirit. But I have lost a lot of her too. In most ways that is a good thing. We cannot move forward while holding on to dead weight from the past. I have learned a lot about patience and timing and trusting things to work out as they should. I have adjusted the ways I view the world, the people I allow in it, and the motivation behind the things for which my heart so eagerly yearns.

But here I am, 5 years later...still a hopeless little dreamer with stars in my eyes, fire in my soul and a burning lust in my belly for all the big dreams I have yet to accomplish and still, without a doubt, believe I will.

becoming

Sleepless nights and Pussy reclamation...

I am loud and messy. I feel deeply and love unconditionally. To many I may seem a difficult woman, but to the right one I know I'll be easy.

And I am emotional, though for years I tried all I could not to be. It used to feel unspeakable, now it's the only way I can set my soul free.

My body was not made for the basic bliss of copulation. I need to connect down to your core, sync to the rhythm of your root vibration.

If I want you, I am all in. If it's love, it's forever. For light or dark, worse or for better.

My sights, once set, are unremitting. My heart, once offered, undoubtedly surrendered. But I won't chase another that does not want to be held, nor sacrifice my honour for the sake of someone else.

I cannot give my world to be hidden or put on a shelf. And if the same is not returned, I have no problem choosing myself.

If your soul is not deep, by me it will not be felt.

I will not wade your shallow waters, seduce me with your seas.

I'd do anything for love, to feel it reciprocated without question or uncertainty.

For these words I know I would burn...if only there were a flame as eager to match my intensity.

becoming

A lesson learned over time- walls and boundaries are great for protecting your heart and shielding from the bad-but they also keep out the good, the beauty and the possibility of growth. Maybe I wasn't being hurt...but I wasn't healing either.

There's only so much expansion you can do on your own...

I feel like I have been living with only half my heart. Wishing to thrive while struggling to barely get by. I want to be open, honest and whole. Not a mere shadow of who I am. To live full and alive in all my essence and share it with the world fearlessly.

Gone are the days of playing small and stifling my voice when I want to scream.

I am full of love.
I want to share it whether it should be reciprocated or not. I want to be. I want to live as all that I am and offer all I have without doubt, shame, blame or belittling.

This is me world. In all her glory. Bask in my flames or retreat…that is up to you. I am done dimming myself.

I have been blaming men and the world and bad love for this for so long, but I call bullshit!!

It is me; it is my own fault. I have chosen to put up walls, to keep love out, to fear and question it and hide from the world. I cannot receive the love I desire until or unless I choose to BECOME it.

So here I am baby…going all in, full throttle, no holding back.

Gonna let my love show.

becoming

I am all heart; I always have been. I got hurt so many times I thought maybe I should start listening to my head instead. To protect myself from the pain others could inflict. In the end, I only ended up hurting myself. Denying myself who I am, ignoring integral parts of me, swallowing my soul and shielding my heart. It keeps the hurt out, but it also blocks love from coming in.

And here I have been, frustrated, spinning my wheels, wondering why I cannot find anyone to love me
...but I was not open to it.

I have never been one to love lightly...

Once I let you under my skin, you remain in my soul, in the beating of my blood and breadth of my bones.

Carried with me in all that I do, the thoughts I think and the way I move.
Eternally altered by the lingering effects of you.

If I have loved you at all, I'll never be done or fully through. To say it, I meant it...and will forever continue to.

becoming

Yesterday marked 5 years since I left an unhealthy relationship. I celebrated. Five years of freedom, independence, growing, learning, and finding myself. But I also mourned a little.

For the girl I was then. The things I allowed and the ways in which I betrayed myself; giving someone the power to slowly chip away at my sense of self, take my generosity for granted, deplete my confidence and destroy me emotionally until there was nothing left but a shell of a woman.

A girl who loved someone so much she disrespected and dishonoured herself to please and appease another. Putting their needs, comforts and desires above hers and wondering why she felt so alone, resentful, bitter and worthless.

I have spent a lot of time mending these broken bits. Picking up the pieces and putting myself back together.

It could be easy to look back with hatred and regret. Push it down or wish it all away…but I do not. I am thankful for all it taught me, and I recognize my part in the hurting and healing. I could never regret anything that has made me the woman I have become.

A woman who knows her worth, loves herself without question, has an unshakeable sense of herself and her values, and will not settle for anything less than she knows she deserves.

A woman who embraces her sensitivity without shame, expresses herself freely and authentically and fearlessly chases her dreams.

To some I may seem difficult, I know. I could be called crazy, emotional, demanding or ridiculous… But I have no problem being considered a "difficult woman" or any other of these things, for that matter.

In fact, it is a point of pride.

To anyone out there reading and relating to my five years ago self…I dare you to stand in your light, demand your worth, and get a little more damn difficult.

kat strain

Foolish little kitty, always falling in love with fantasies
Building them up in her brain and convincing herself they are meant to be
Then left to take the fall when things aren't as they seem

Will I ever find a love I do not have to create in my dreams?

Better start with a little more care and a little less curiosity
Accept what is actually there and leave my imagination to stories for screens

becoming

I am poetry and she is free pornography.

You are unable to discern which holds more value…

kat strain

One comes in soft and slow, growing over time with a depth and beauty that is breathtaking and everlasting.

But requires patience.

The other is hot and fast, with an intensity that blinds but wears off once you realize behind it there's no substance.

It never lasts.

All things that shimmer surely fade in time.
Even diamonds lose their lustre to adjusted eyes.

If you want heat and passion, you must build a fire, stoke its flames and do the work to keep it burning.

That's the thing about desire...it is built through the establishment of deep trust and emotional intimacy.

Lust exists easily, but it is fleeting.
A poor and pitiful conduit for true heat.

And when it cools and wears out, it'll leave you on your knees.

Deplete.

Empty handed, broken hearted, and praying for the promise of poetry.

becoming

If desire equated love, I'd know not the deep sting of loneliness.

As a woman, I have felt desired without fail every day since I became one.
But loved…fully and truly, as I am, for exactly who I am…not once.

I am an ever-hungry heart seeking the satiation of love and slowly starving on the lacklustre breadcrumbs of lust. No amount could ever appease me, no depth or density of desire alone would leave me full.

In fact, it is a trick I could do without completely.
A mere shadow of what I crave.
A perilous tease that leaves me feeling empty.

Like lukewarm embers of a flickering flame when I long to be consumed by an infernos rage.

In moments like this I am not entirely sad, but I wish to be filled with the kind of joy that would only be found in the promise of a lover, the hope for tomorrow, a future to be filled.

A person to climb into bed with and wake up to in the morning, arms to hold me tight and the bliss of being truly in love and loved in return.

But tonight, I go to bed alone.
Empty armed, hopeless and knowing I will wake to the same fate.

For now…but tonight that feels like forever.

Merry Christmas.

becoming

Just me to me...

I am proud of you for choosing to keep your heart open and feel when it would be so much easier to simply shut it off or close it down.

It will destroy you later, if you do not let it hurt now.

I know you've been here before, your heart no stranger to a losing score.

You called it resilience and ignored the pain in the past to prove you moved on faster.

Convinced yourself it did not matter...but it does.

It did then, and still does somehow.

So, feel it baby, let it all out.

Rest and recover so it doesn't come back around to wreck your world and completely tear you down.

It's okay to accept it's just going to hurt for now.

Have patience with yourself
and stay soft.

Don't you dare let this callous
or close you off.

If your heart can break,
that means it's still beating.

The deeper the pain, the further
the depths to which you are capable of feeling.

And that kind of love, my darling, is a feat to be truly proud of.

I feel such a deep sadness in my soul nothing will shake.
I can only accept and honour it.
An unwelcome burden I am used to surmounting with ease but cannot seem to find the strength.
I cannot recall the last time I felt so down for so long…I fear it might never leave.

becoming

I am slowly sinking into my softness...it is new terrain.
I haven't been here so fully in longer than I can recall. But it is warm and
welcoming and feels like coming home.

It is also heart wrenching and heartbreaking to be so open to feel.
The hurt, the pain, the sadness consumes me some days,
but I wouldn't trade it away.
I could never again return to my hard and cold ways.

Living half alive is not living...I'd rather crash and burn than never feel at all.

*This year I want to greet every day with a heart so full and open,
the world won't know what to do with it.*

No more guarding or hiding away.

*I'm offering only a whole lotta love in hopes, perhaps,
one day a little might also come back my way.*

becoming

My heart has spent a lifetime shackled by the strictures of fear
It begs to beat and bleed freely the bounty of its boundless love
To ravish and rush as fiercely as these waves

Fearless.

Reckless.

Wild and undone.

She is ready to risk it all and looking for the one
Who will drown in her depths, no care to be saved
Gladly walk beside her, hand in hand in the rain
Warm her bones with the ferocity of their flames
For that kind of love she'd endure any pain
Brave every storm and bear the seas seething rage

The first and only thing I have ever written about my sexual assault in LA. I buried it a long time, not wanting to accept or look it in the face. But it broiled beneath my skin and sabotaged everything in its wake until I finally acknowledged, admitted and granted it sweet release from my soul. I hate the sense of shame that surrounds this, I hate the knowledge that this experience is also, so sadly, not in the slightest unique to me. It disgusts me to know most reading will likely relate.

I beg you to shout and scream and set yourself free...do not dare let some spineless coward seal your fate!

becoming

I have spent years trying to reclaim my body. To restore the purity and passion of this sacred land, which was seized and spoiled by the thoughtless actions of a selfish man.

Overthinking where I used to be uninhibited. Calculated instead of carefree.
In truth, I will never return to that state. To that girl. She no longer exists.
But I hope I am building a better, stronger version. One who can use her discernment to honour and protect herself while still finding ways to submit to her softness and sensuality...and eventually, effortlessly express and experience her fire to its fullest.

It is a journey which frustrates me often. One so many women must make, though none should ever have to.

But someday I'm sure I will feel the stirrings and with them no shame. Be able to share myself without fear or pain. And trust past transgressions shall not happen to me again.

Rejoice rather than recoil at the firm touch of another and cherish the sanctity of sharing my body with a safe and soulful lover.

I know I give off this image of a hard and strong, super independent woman...

But I've actually always been a very soft and sensitive soul searching for deep connection and unconditional love.

The calloused façade is the armour I've built over time to shield and protect my bruised and battered heart.

I'd love to find someone safe enough to lay it all down. A home that holds me close and allows me to embrace rather than hide my softness.

I long to sheath my sword and sweetly surrender to the heart and arms of a soul soft enough to share, honour and return my sensitivities.

becoming

I watch as the tide softly trickles in
Like the trail of hot tears stinging my skin
Stirring my emotions, striking a chord deep within
Cascading along the shore before being swept back whence they came
Reminding me, however subtle the change…
Nothing in life can forever remain the same

Just as the ice outlining the bank will melt back into the soil
And the flock of ducks now drift beyond the rocks out of sight
Time is ever fleeting and at some point, we all must leave
What comes must go again, we all float on eventually
So mollify me with your melody and the dissonant song of the geese
For now, a bitter moment, a sweet reverie and sorrows release

kat strain

For my Tibby boy...an ode to the "love of my life" – a big hearted, oversized orange tabby cat I adopted at age 20, who slept with me religiously and looked at me with more love than I've ever felt from a pair of human eyes.

becoming

Anyone who knows me, knows the extent of my deep bond
with this beautiful little beast

My little spoon, my sweet boy, my baby, my Chippy

I love you endlessly

He saw me through all of my 20's, my toughest trials and greatest joys
Many moves and many moods, full of affection and never far from my side

My heart is heavy today, my eyes swim with this goodbye
A weighted sadness in my soul that shall linger a lengthy time

I longed to hold on dearly, but let you go with grace
Gone now but never forgotten, nor could ever be replaced

The end came all too quickly and regretfully filled with pain
No matter what I wished, I could not take away

There will always be a hole in my heart where your memory remains
There I'll carry you forever and continue to cherish the love you gave

~Every sorrow I have known in my adult life has been cradled by this kitty and cried into his fur. I feel sick with sadness now, but I will be truly lost tonight with no place for these tears to land~

Early this morning I followed him downstairs when he left my bed. Knowing we had only mere hours yet to share each others presence. I sat quietly with him, stroking his fur and taking in the rise of the dawn... ruminating that we just never know how many we will get and when will be our last. And with that, how imperative it is to make the most of each moment. To live bravely and boldly and leave nothing to regret.

So, in honour of Chippy I invite you to join me in this promise...

To take a chance, take the risk, stop making excuses and book that trip. Eat the treats, share a kiss, and bask in the warmth of the sun on your skin. Love hard and deeply, say so as often as you can and always take full advantage of every dawn with which you are blessed.

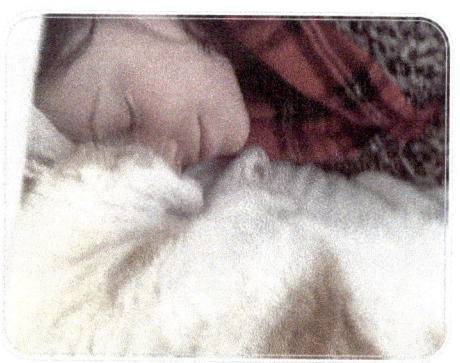

becoming

Sometimes after an intense workout I close my eyes in silent meditation while I catch my breath and let my mind wander...

Recently I had a vision of myself "becoming". My toes tethered to the earth but bound by no limits, my stem extending from the soles as I twist and twist upward towards the sun. My arms outstretched above my head, slowly opening, relaxing, releasing as I rise. From tight bud to beautifully blossomed lotus flower. Naked, free, unashamed. Chest toward the skies, head thrown back, wild hair askew in the breeze. My heart, radiant, a shining beacon of love and light pouring out endlessly on all around it. Not a person or particle left untouched. I am not seen, nor judged, but I am felt. A warm glow of soothing light as I continue to spin. Basking in all that I am and all that I have become. Like a windup fairy toy ready to take flight, or a ballerina pirouetting in a music box.

I've never felt more free...more myself than I have ever been.

Being in love alone is the loneliest place a person can find themselves.

Nothing can fill that kind of void or sooth such a startling ache.

To love and be loved in return, what a gift.

To me, it seems, an unreachable feat.

becoming

Sailboats, sunshine and sensitivity...

I found my North off the coast of Barcelona as I sat swaying in a sailboat. Eyes close, face towards the sun. The salty spray striking my face and breeze billowing through my hair. My heart enlarged, happy and full. I rested in my knowing. Everything was about to change for the better. My time had come. She was home.

I am no diamond.

I am a vintage emerald, a priceless heirloom passed down from generations before. Full of history, passion and poetry. Full of hope and dreams and endless unexpected opportunity.
Rare, unique, irreplicable and irreplaceable. An acquired taste, perhaps, but I have stories to share, can offer the world, and I am timeless. I may not shine as bright at first glance, but I will not tarnish or lose my lustre.

I will never be a diamond. I have no wish to be. I've no taste for them.

So, if a diamond is truly what you seek, then I am not for you.

I will never sparkle enough.

But to another I will hold much greater value and be held sacred and dear. Cherished and honoured as the most precious stone they have ever seen.

In certain moments, I felt you looked at me as though an emerald was all you could ever dream. Those moments still haunt me.

That is what makes this so difficult to accept.

But I must.

becoming

Sometimes when you reflect on someone you loved so intensely, you realize that love was actually yours! It always came from and belonged to you...not them. They did not provide it and so they could not ever steal it away!!

Today my heart is like a well after a heavy flood
Brimming, bursting, overflowing with love and gratitude

For myself, for my life...for the one on which I wait,
who must also be waiting for me

For the sheer depth and existence of this love that beats in my body
The ways in which it stirs my blood, warms my bones, and fills me with joy

A moody morning and a watery walk...

I always find myself near the water.

When I am lost and uncertain. On grey days when I cannot recall why I am here or what it is all for... when sadness fills my soul and shallows my breath... when the feelings I carry are too big for my body to bear...

I toss them to the waves and watch them roll away, reveling in their release
I face my body to the breeze, and it forces me to go deep
The waters rage and yet my heart finds peace

I feel akin with the clouds as both of our tears slide down my cheek

I whisper my worries to the wind and always receive the wisdom I seek

On days like today the surest way to breathe life back into this battered soul is a walk on the beach

becoming

These country roads have brought me home, back to the place I call my own

Not in the house, nor city I live, but all abound within this skin

Birthday bikini bravery...

becoming

Hey, this is me!

I am almost 33.
In the last 5 years my body has changed tremendously.

At times I look in the mirror and feel confused by this version I see.
I work out 5 days a week and do my best to eat healthy.

But I also enjoy a large glass of wine, a few beers in the sunshine, cake when the occasion is right and pizza on a Friday night.

No limitations, no shame, nothing I cannot do, or wear based on the breadth of my frame. No shushing my voice or hiding in the shadows, the spotlight I'll reclaim.

My value has not lessened with each pound of flesh I have gained.
I am woman. I am goddess.
And the world will know my name.

~I will live freely and fiercely, for I am here to take up space~

kat strain

The moon and me are very good friends...

We both shine when the lights dim, our lonely-hearts beckoning
At peace in our solitude, but ever reaching
No dark corner to which our light cannot extend
Wither to nothing at times, concealing our soul
But without fail always building back again

Hazy or clear, half, quarter, clip or full
We soothe, we lull, our presence ever intendedly peaceful

Longing for the sun, for our darkness to be done
To still be seen and felt when the lights come on

becoming

After years of hoping, praying, and planning for that "someday", I finally took on my biggest feat yet. In four months time, from conception to picture wrap, my sister and I funded/produced/wrote/directed and starred in our first feature film. A dream held sacred in our hearts through the decades of our struggles in the industry.

A dream we were at one time convinced we must go anywhere else in the world to accomplish, and must require financial support and the help and expertise of others to achieve...now made possible solely due to the fact that we returned home, put our heads down, realigned our vision, saved some money and stopped making excuses for ourselves/outsourcing others to do what we could on our own.

The experience was a dream come true. The most exhilarating and challenging of our lives. It consumed us both many months and left little room for any other consideration or creativity. I wrote this after a long week of filming, sitting under the moonlight, realizing I hadn't written anything personal in quite some time.

You've laid dormant in me so long, simmering below the surface.

Your steady stream held stagnant by the static of my mind.

At times I fear you will not return, yet ever intuit the faintest shadow of your essence.

Melding with my own.

Aching.

Longing to be heard.

To be freed.

I shall return to you soon...will you wait for me?

Linger in my depths, prepare for our sweet release.

The beauty of that experience fed and fueled the fires of my soul and heart, leaving me feeling limitless and unstoppable...but my body bore the brunt and would soon inform me of its very real and inflexible limits.

The stress of producing a feature film with $40,000 and a 2-person team landed me in the hospital with a very severe colitis flare up- a disease I previously had no idea raged so fiercely inside of me. The 2 weeks I spent in the hospital, struggling to survive on broth and sleepless nights, were the most painful, terrifying and eye opening of my entire life.

Learning to accept, treat and readjust to this disease and all its symptoms would be the shock my system needed to reset and take stock of the poor choices I had continued to carry from my past which were dishonouring my body and holding me back.

Your new life will always cost you your old and I was finally ready to shed that skin, restore and be rebirthed. Chrysalis to butterfly, that thought is what got me through this troubling time. The following pieces I like to call my "prednisone poetry".

The steroid that saved my life and kept me up at night can be attributed to the influx of writing that flowed from me in the small hours of dawn for many months.

becoming

Sleepless steroid mornings...

I spent days with all my demons recently
They told me who I was and who I aught to be

I had first to wrestle before they offered me release
Learn to stand again after being brought to my knees

Had to accept the fault and fate of their disease
Wallowed through my depths and fought my darkness to be freed

The cost was considerable, nearly impossible to conceive
But left no other choice than to willingly concede

I held myself, I cried, I felt broken and bereaved
Said goodbye to all I've been and lovingly took my leave

Burned it all to the ground and left no morsel to retrieve
So I can build it all again, stronger, better, piece by piece

I have always considered myself a formidable figure.
Taken pride in my physical strength.

I battled a health scare recently that has tested and taken this from me.
Stripping me of my cherished autonomy.

I hardly recognize myself. I feel foreign in my skin.
My form once thick with muscles, now left frail and thin.

We do not recognize how much we take our health for granted,
until it is compromised.

I am battling a chronic disease that will follow me indefinitely.
But if I am truly honest, this didn't just happen to me.
I fed it for years by dishonouring my body.

Dismissing the symptoms, ignoring the warning signs and
assuming it would always be just fine.

I should be packing my bags, days away from boarding a plane.
To my much-anticipated Scottish highland hide away.

A writing retreat I dreamed of for years and planned/paid for 6 months ago.
Another thing this illness forced me to surrender and let go.

The last few months have been the toughest of my life.
Cost me considerably, caused a lot of strife.

Robbed my body but granted a new lease on life.
A softening of my soul, a humbling, a chance to think twice.
A toughening of my mind and an opportunity to get things right.

I can rebuild my muscles, unbreak my heart and rebook my trip...but my body will keep this score.

You can be damn sure I will pay whatever price necessary to never find myself here again. All we truly have is our health in the end.

Do not take it for granted, friends.

becoming

I have an insatiable hunger in my heart...

It claws at my chest and consumes my soul
At times I fear it could swallow me whole

I yearn, I crave, I long, I lust
Yet empty of hand, it is never enough
For unconditional, all encompassing, deep and devoted love
For success and accomplishment...just out of reach,
my dreams dangle above

Am I delusional?
Do I pine for too much?

Will I ever be satisfied, full or complete?
How long must I wait for all my wants to meet?
No matter how far I roam, I forever itch at my feet
Nor how much I hold, my hands feel deplete

This longing leaves me weary
Lofty lusting drives me mad
Eternally unquenched, no matter the lot or little I've had

Do I dare dream too big?
Does this burning make me bad?

Am I destined to be restless...an ever-searching lonely nomad?

~The forever frustration of being unable to adequately describe the depths of my distraught~

Yesterday my mother told me she was taken by the sight of a single leaf falling from the barren trees outside her window. She considered it a pity I was not present to witness and capture it in a poem.

It seems my mind intuited the imagery, regardless, as these words came to me moments before sleep...

I watch with bated breath as you make your slow descent to the earth

Swaying, swirling, suspended in time

I am caught, enchanted, mesmerized

A free fall from your comfort zone, a trusted leap to the unknown
You follow those before you, but your journey is your own

The last one to leave, your stubbornness has shown
But each autumn precedes a winter, and now it's time to go

So, twist and turn and take your time
I shan't dare miss the show

I will honour your final moments...a fated flight to the floor below

becoming

I want to let go...of all of it.

Every tether that has tied me down and shackled me to my past.

Every missed opportunity, every undeserved heartache, every low effort love that never equated to my deserved depth.

I want to shed these sheaths that have kept me small, silenced my inner knowing, convinced me I am unworthy.

No longer will I accept anything less than my value, all I desire, and everything meant for me.

To anyone/thing planning to enter my orbit...admission ain't free.

Meet me at my frequency, or kindly concede.

Purged after a bonus intestinal infection and severe bout of anemia...

The deeper the darkness I traverse, the lighter I become.

Even the most beastly of life's challenges offer some vestige of beauty...if you listen, if you really look, if you stay open when you want to close, crack when you crave to callous, and find the love in lack.

Sometimes life separates us, isolates us, drags and beats us down...strips us of all we have and know, the safety of our comfort zone.

Lost, lonely and listless we must search for ourselves in the rubble. For the root, the core, the truest and most honest bits and start again.

Stronger, better and with clearer intent.

~Home from a second stint in the hospital. Sometimes things must get worse before they get better...but I am back on the mend and more hopeful than ever~

becoming

I saw something yesterday that stirred these words in my soul. How men are often drawn to free spirited women. They admire, yet long to possess her. In doing so, destroying and diminishing the very qualities which lured them.

~You say you love me but put me in a cage~

Starve me of air and steal my light
No mind it could kill me to be kept shut tight
It's my freedom you crave, yet fear I'll take flight
Onto bigger and better and leave you in blight
So, you clip my wings and watch with delight
Your creature, your prize, your worldly right
Unwill my wild spirit just to keep me in sight

Until I am broken and void of the very zest you admire
Grounded, barren, listless and uninspired
A soulless shadow once fiercely afire
A wounded bird of which you'll grow tired
A foiled fate of the dream you conspired
A lacklustre shell of a once striking sapphire
You'll set me free, move on, and respire

~For she no longer soars or sings upon your wire~

kat strain

I find you dazed hours of dawn...you haunt restless remembering in the eve
Through eyes firmly fixed, with wondering whispers you weave
I ponder how you've been and if you ever think of me
Whether you are better off and find yourself happy
I bless the divinity and do my best to set you free
But it seems my heady heart and head disagree
I lose moments to hours in this rife reverie
No peace, so solace, faint relief or reprieve
Each night, without fail, I meet my tormenting thief
My repose abated by our delirious debrief
As I struggle to slumber, you drift in with ease
And steal the sacred spaces betwixt awake and asleep

becoming

This one kept me up many, many hours to fully articulate and organize but frankly sums up my disdain for patriarchal gender expectations and so must have been brewing in my soul much longer than the mere hours of this eve...

Your mission in life, find a man to make you wife
Settle down, be smart, don't stress or strife

Build babies, not careers, they will become your whole life
Bring you purpose and worth and ease your plight

Shoulder the weight of the world, but tuck your worries out of sight
Don't dare raise your voice, even when you are right

Don't be brave or bold, no battle is worth the blight
A man will surely save you, do not waste all your might

But be soft and warm, you're only loved for your light
Even when you're worn out, better keep burning bright

When outwilled or wronged, don't dare show contempt
Smooth your hair, paint your face, and keep your nails well kempt

Put your best on display, you were born to impress
To be pretty, polite, docile and voiceless

Your passions and dreams are time ill spent
Drop such foolish follies and live solely for their success

Always minimize yourself to maximize the rest
Never raise your tone, nor push or press

You'll bleed every month, but better hide your mess
It is dirty and disgusting and makes you less attractive

kat strain

Carry your secrets and shame, there's no need to confess
You'll be a burden to others, only cause to oppress

It is vile and rude to show a man disrespect
Be sweet and submissive, you're the fairer sex

And when it comes to your body you must afford full access
If you aren't perceived as meek, you'll be considered monstrous

You exist to please, don't think twice just undress
Even if you disagree, better acquiesce

Commit your life, your freedom and full faithfulness
And when they take you for granted do not fuss or fret

When faced with opposition you must always digress
Keep your opinions to yourself, you've nothing worthy to express

Don't be clever or coy, spare the world your inconsequential quips
Ironic then, we should be born with two sets of lips

becoming

Another sleepless night inspired some words to write in recollection of an earlier sight...

I savour the soft caress of the evening sun on my skin
Take the moment to curl up beside my languid furry friend
Both dimming our dazzled eyes, the wondrous warmth spreads within
Pure pleasure fills our souls as the seconds seem to suspend
I am safe, I am serene, so sweetly cradled in my bed
Knowing clouds will surely come, but you shall shine on me until then
I will revel this blanket of rays your generosity extends
And hold this moment in my heart until we three meet here again

kat strain

I must feel things deeply to be compelled to write
Inspired and impassioned by a thought or sight

Emblazoned by emotion, be it dark or be it light
Whether it fills me with compassion or leaves me cold and contrite

My heart an open canvas, my pen its wings a flight
I surrender to its siege, my hand it heeds with sheer delight

becoming

I am finally surrendering to the softness
that has always stirred within me.
Finding safety in the sweetness of my soul.
Embracing it fully and sharing it freely.

Unencumbered by the past and all the thorns that calloused me.
Shedding that tough skin, unsheathing my heart within,
choosing love and living fearlessly.

Bless the divinity...I cannot miss out on what's meant for me.
All else, I let go of gracefully.

~I've spent years crafting and curating for myself a life of art and poetry~

A perspective I'd dare not trade for anything, though it seems, at times, more a curse than a blessing. I cannot help but see the beauty in everything. Both good and bad, warranted or undeserving.

A gift that fills me to brimming just as often as it leaves me empty.

These eyes can find light in even the darkest of night.
Where many will fold is when I find my inner fight.
Once I set my soul, the sparks ignite.

~I am all in, devoted, be it blessing or blight~

becoming

A lesson I have learned in life and love repeatedly...
only go or stay where you are valued.

I only want what wants me, as wholehearted and passionately.

Anything less or other, I will happily set free.

I look at the soft red glow of my flickering candle lit room. The shadowed silhouettes it cascades in a silent moving picture, sip my spiced tea in solitude, and am utterly convinced my life is filled to brimming with romance, magic and poetry.

And so, it shall always be.

becoming

I'll no longer shrivel and shrink under the weight of judgement and shame.
I have shed the shackles of societal expectations and surrendered to my sovereignty.

Now see me soar.

Another round of the previous infection and persistent anemia symptoms prompt a warning from my doctor that the next viable option, should we continue to see such lack of improvement to my condition, would be surgery. Made clear that the severity of my case would likely require the removal of my entire colon, not just part...a reality I will not and could never accept for myself. I still held hope but had to use the best outlet I know to release my fear...

I am just fucking sad and scared today. I feel like I have lost enough and no matter how much I try to grasp and find gratitude with where I am, I cannot catch my footing. More keeps slipping and sliding away. I cannot get ahead.

When is it enough? When have I given enough, learned enough? Lost enough? Is there no end? Am I destined to slip and slide and suffer and never find myself on steady ground?

Do I deserve no love to hold my hand through these trials, no shoulder on which to relieve this burden I must continue to carry on my own? No sympathy, no solace, no reprieve?

I want to leave this behind. A distant memory I will honour and warning I will heed. Move onto greener pastures healthy and whole and look back fondly for all it taught me and the person it built. I don't want to be in this anymore...struggling, gasping, questioning and losing little pieces of myself, relentlessly.

I am not prepared to part with anymore. Especially not the parts in question.

And I am angry. At all the things that got me here. A casual diagnosis at 27 with no follow up, no treatment and no care...the years this festered inside of me unaware, and the cruel ways I treated and took for granted my body...thinking myself young and invincible. Not knowing I was slowly destroying parts of myself I now wish dearly I could fix, return to a state of health and never again cause harm.

becoming

I am angry it's too late and I cannot go back. That the damage is done. I can't shut my eyes and will it away. And maybe time can heal...but it has already been six months and I am beginning to lose patience and hope...and more and more and MORE of my goddamn hair. And it saddens and terrifies me. I am frustrated and stricken with grief.

The only way through is acceptance. Over which I am tongue tied, tripping and cannot seem to manage with grace.

But tomorrow is another day.

kat strain

Fall had its way with my heart and winter tore this body apart.

Spring be sweet to me...please.

becoming

I lay in bed the small hours of dawn listening to the rain.
Wide awake and filled with peace.
Watching shadows play along my wall and reveling in the choir of bird song.

The sky slowly lightens while trees sway across my bookcase,
my room a wondrous reflection of my mind...
a show of shadowed silhouette.

I know the sun will soon rise and steal my pensive state, and so I savour it.

Surrendering myself to the secrets of each sated second.

Through all of my trials and setbacks I kept my mind strong and positive, and my body followed. Building strength over time and slowly returning to my once active state...

> I love long, early morning, languid country walks
> A soft breeze, some birds and geese, and me
>
> So peaceful and quiet, I can hear myself think
> My mind wanders while being led by my feet
> The surest sense I have ever felt of peace
> Whatever the weather, I am comfortable and complete

> My soul symphony hums along to the choir of nature's song...
> and together, we make beautiful music

becoming

~poet heart, artist eye, and storyteller soul~

The down time and isolation were a beautiful gift, granting me plenty of time to look deep within, get clear about who I was, what I wanted and how I could bring it all to fruition. The opportunity to hear my voice even clearer than before and to honour and celebrate it in ways I never had. Clarifying my passion and purpose in life and offering a much different, deeper and more encompassing perspective.

I started checking off my list of hopeful accomplishments…no more limitations, no more excuses. This butterfly was ready to stretch her wings. A new woman had been born and I was totally and utterly in love with her.

God, I love this girl!!

Her heart and soul and brain…and all the beautiful fucking creativity that flows through these veins!

becoming

I used to search for poems and songs to show me the words poignant enough to express how I feel...but could never quite find any adequate.

So, I decided I must create them.

Now I hope to bring that clarity to others.

I am finally, fully certified to instruct boxing!

It is a goal I started at the age of 26 when I decided to take my training more seriously with a boxing club. I knew, given my other work, I'd never step foot in a ring... but I wanted to say I could, to know if I did, I could hold my own.

This goal was extended and put off through multiple moves and different coaches in Toronto, LA and then Chatham. Life got in the way, but still it burned in me.

Growing up I was painfully shy. Always the "good girl", doing as I was told, staying "in line", overachieving and appeasing. Keeping my mouth shut and never ever wanting to cause a problem or make a fuss. I carried this into adulthood. Until I finally realized, midway through my 20's this had never and certainly no longer served me, but kept me small, scared and taken for granted.

Boxing burnt this damn for me. Built the sense of pride, confidence and self esteem I long craved and wished I could possess. It lit a fire in me I was previously unaware smouldered in my depths. I decided quickly I wanted to learn to teach, so I could share that feeling with other women. But it started more so as a possible job avenue to get me out of my serving grind.

Over the years, this desire ebbed and flowed depending on other circumstances my life presented... but the goal and the reasoning behind it would only deepen and clarify.

I have found my truest and most authentic voice the last years. As a woman and as an artist. Anyone who knows me, knows I am not afraid to use it;)

My passion and purpose in life have combined to show me I am here to use my voice to uplift the voices of those still scared to speak and hiding in the shadows. Almost everything I do is fueled by my drive to educate and empower women. To encourage them to reclaim their power, stand confidently in their skin, take up space in this world and fearlessly speak their truth.

becoming

I love women. I love working for and with them.

But I realized… the best way to help women, is to start at the source. Girls. What if we started teaching our little girls to naturally be bold, brave, fearless and confident. They would become woman who do not need empowerment to be their most brilliant and radiant selves!!

This is a big feat, and I am merely one woman!!! But I can offer what I know and do something…
anything.

And so, a few summers ago, *Soul Strong* was conceived with my sister, Karissa. A workshop program we'd like to start in town for young women. To learn a skill that will encourage body confidence, self esteem, strength and empowerment… and hopefully and most importantly sistership!!

I know, if we can be even a small shift in but one girl's life towards achieving the sense of self worth and courage it took us many years and countless setbacks, stumbles and difficult lessons to accomplish, this will be worth every penny and all the hard work!!

13–16-year-old ladies of Chatham Kent… step into our ring.

Let's wrap those wrists and take a swing.

I saw my grandfather a few days ago. I sat and chatted with him a bit and he asked what I'd been up to. He was surprised when I mentioned I was planning a boxing workshop for girls in town. "Are you a boxer?" he asked, slightly astounded, "I didn't know that." About me he knows very little. "Yes" I said, "I think it is very important young women be encouraged to pursue activities that are deemed masculine."

He gave me a sideways glance, chuckled and elbowed me lightly as he commented, "you know I don't really agree with you." And for the first time in my life, I did not feel defensive, outraged or rejected. I laughed back, earnestly, and responded, "I have no doubt there is plenty on which we would not agree." Then we let it go and carried on with ease.

For a change I did not care. I didn't bury it down, dissect and overthink it, take offense or let it spoil my mood. I simply accepted our differences and respected his valid opinion while knowing I need not his validation to stand firmly in my own.

It was beautiful and freeing.

His truth took nothing from mine and with not every person, on every topic, must I see eye to eye.

We chatted a little longer and he hugged me as I said goodbye. "Goodluck with your boxing," he offered, a slight glint in his eye.

And I believe, in his own way, he truly meant it.

becoming

I spent hours this morning just laying in bed. Cuddling my cat, enjoying the breeze and listening to the rhythmic sound of the rain outside my window. Practicing the subtle art of "being" and savouring every second.

As women, we feel me must always be "doing" and accomplishing to prove our value, to show our worth. We run ourselves ragged, rarely garnering the recognition it deserves and wonder why we find ourselves filled with resentment and worn out.

Somewhere along the way we seem to have forgotten that our presence is our power. We hold value because we merely exist...just being is enough!

Stop doing so damn much and embrace the beauty of allowing yourself to "be". Set that nervous system at ease and crumple up that list of all you must achieve.

No one is keeping score anyway.

Grab a book, a cup of tea or whatever you damn well please and take some time just for you today.

The kind of clarity that comes from finally being in full alignment with yourself is so freeing...

Like tar filled lungs inhaling clean air amidst years of pollution, or the gift of 20/20 after a lifetime of living blind.

There's no better feeling in the world than discovering your true purpose here and knowing every step you take each and every day is paving the path to getting there.

After staggering astray so many years, it's almost unsettling to feel so stable and grounded.

I may not hold all the answers for my future, but the vision is clear...and to its source I shamelessly surrender.

I am here to empower, embrace and uplift women.
To use my voice to illuminate those still scared to use theirs.

To be confident, bold and brave, have the audacity to take up space and encourage my fellow sisters to do the same.

becoming

It is 7 months since my harrowing health scare, and I am booked for a colonoscopy to determine if treatment is indeed working. Despite the doctors increasing concerns from the inflammation indicated in my previous bloodwork, I am positively expecting good results.

I enjoy some light banter with the witty elderly gentleman who is designated to prepare me for my procedure. He sympathizes with my age and the intensity of my year but appreciates my humour and good spirits.

"I had two sons and two daughters," he says, "and I always used to tell the girls that boys are like buses."

Pausing for dramatic effect while piling my belongings into a locker, I wait for his punchline.

He locks it and continues with a wink, "there's always another one coming."

We share a giggle of agreeance and I shrug in retort… "and sometimes, it's just better to walk!" He is caught off guard by my quick rebuttal and splits a gut, enjoying the sentiment immensely. I can tell he will use this material to brighten the day of future patients and it leaves me pleased.

Meanwhile…my gut is mending nicely. Not quite in remission but well on its way. The light has shown itself at the end of the tunnel and finally it feels within reach.

I am overcome these days, overwhelmed by all these words and the ways in which they find me, fuel me and feed my soul.

I am so proud of who I have become.

A blossoming poet with no shortage of wisdom. These words come to me at night when I am tuned in and turned on. They keep me from sleep but flow with ease and for no feat in the world would I trade or change them.

I am humbled and honoured to call them my own. To know they come from this soul and are mine alone.

They will remain with me forever, the sweetest claim I could ever make. A gift, my truest blessing, a force I'd never forsake.

I should be frustrated and annoyed that I lay in bed awake…but in truth I'd miss them dearly were they to offer me a break.

I find my purest parts those quiet moments in the night. When my mind is open and clear, nothing distracts the voice with which I write.

It is brave, it is bold, it is authentic, and it is mine.
I'd lay sleepless here forever before I'd ever leave it behind.

It is everything I've always dreamed, this ideal I longed to become.
This illusory woman whom I aspired…now seems we've finally joined as one.

about the author

I have always had a passion for expression and storytelling. First through dance, then performance- on stage and on screen. Sharing, emoting and evoking feeling in others stirs my soul. Those mediums allowed me to share the stories and voices of others.

Writing has become a way for me to find and strengthen my own voice and share my stories. It is not a choice, but a compulsion. As natural and essential as breathing.

I feel the urge and I let my pen flow. I never know where or when it might consume me. Sometimes I'm not even sure whose words they are and if they are indeed of my own heart. Regardless, I am an eager and grateful conduit. I am a highly passionate, overly sensitive, hopeless romantic brimming with thoughts and emotions and a deep, desperate need to purge them.

Were I to swallow them down, ignoring their urge and denying myself their release into the world, I'm quite convinced I might just burst.

Poetry is both my salvation and damnation. My biggest strength and surest weakness.
My shameful sorrow and purest joy.

Every particle that beats within my skin brought to the surface, My pulse, my heart...my soul's true purpose.

www.ingramcontent.com/pod-product-compliance
Lightning Source LLC
Chambersburg PA
CBHW041036020526
44118CB00043BA/2999